NAVAL WAR COLLEGE
Newport, R.I.

MARITIME OPERATIONAL THREAT RESPONSE CENTER:

THE MISSING PIECE IN THE
NATIONAL STRATEGY FOR MARITIME SECURITY

by

John J. Gordon

Commander, USN

A paper submitted to the Faculty of the Naval War College in partial satisfaction of the requirements of the Department of Joint Military Operations.

Signature: _____

16 May 2006

REPORT DOCUMENTATION PAGE

1. REPORT DATE (DD-MM-YYYY) 16-05-2006	2. REPORT TYPE FINAL	3. DATES COVERED (From - To)

4. TITLE AND SUBTITLE	5a. CONTRACT NUMBER
A Maritime Operational Threat Response Center: The Missing Piece in the National Strategy for Maritime Security	
	5b. GRANT NUMBER
	5c. PROGRAM ELEMENT NUMBER

6. AUTHOR(S)	5d. PROJECT NUMBER
CDR John J. Gordon	5e. TASK NUMBER
Paper Advisor (if Any): Ivan Luke	5f. WORK UNIT NUMBER

7. PERFORMING ORGANIZATION NAME(S) AND ADDRESS(ES)	8. PERFORMING ORGANIZATION REPORT NUMBER
Joint Military Operations Department Naval War College 686 Cushing Road Newport, RI 02841-1207	

9. SPONSORING/MONITORING AGENCY NAME(S) AND ADDRESS(ES)	10. SPONSOR/MONITOR'S ACRONYM(S)
	11. SPONSOR/MONITOR'S REPORT NUMBER(S)

12. DISTRIBUTION / AVAILABILITY STATEMENT
Distribution Statement A: Approved for public release; Distribution is unlimited.

13. SUPPLEMENTARY NOTES A paper submitted to the faculty of the NWC in partial satisfaction of the requirements of the JMO Department. The contents of this paper reflect my own personal views and are not necessarily endorsed by the NWC or the Department of the Navy.

14. ABSTRACT

The United States is developing a unified strategy to manage Maritime Security. The task requires coordination of a number of U.S. Government agencies and coalition partners. The Maritime Operational Threat Response plan is designed to coordinate the response across the multiple agencies. Coordination of the response to a Maritime Operational Threat is done via virtual collaboration across the MOTR agencies. This organizational arrangement is less than optimal. The United States requires a single operational command center to synthesis, coordinate, and direct the operational response to threats in the Maritime Domain. This paper describes the advantages of a Maritime Operational Threat Response Center to coordinate the response to threats from the Maritime Domain.

15. SUBJECT TERMS
Maritime Security; Maritime Domain Awareness, Terrorism, Interagency Cooperation

16. SECURITY CLASSIFICATION OF:			17. LIMITATION OF ABSTRACT	18. NUMBER OF PAGES	19a. NAME OF RESPONSIBLE PERSON Chairman, JMO Dept
a. REPORT UNCLASSIFIED	b. ABSTRACT UNCLASSIFIED	c. THIS PAGE UNCLASSIFIED		23	19b. TELEPHONE NUMBER (include area code) 401-841-3556

Abstract

The United States is developing a unified strategy to manage Maritime Security. The task requires coordination of a number of U.S. Government agencies and coalition partners. The Maritime Operational Threat Response plan is designed to coordinate the response across the multiple agencies. Coordination of the response to a Maritime Operational Threat is done via virtual collaboration across the MOTR agencies. This organizational arrangement is less than optimal. The United States requires a single operational command center to synthesis, coordinate, and direct the operational response to threats in the Maritime Domain. This paper describes the advantages of a Maritime Operational Threat Response Center to coordinate the response to threats from the Maritime Domain.

Table of Contents

INTRODUCTION

The United States is vulnerable to attack from the Maritime Domain. With the world's largest economy, highly dependent on global trade, the United States stands to suffer significant loss from a terrorist attack from the sea. 95% of overseas trade moves through the nation's port shipping system.[1] Disruption of this shipping system can have dire consequences to the U.S. economy. In a war game conducted by Booz Allen Hamilton and The Conference Board in 2002, the impact to the U.S. economy of a modest terrorist attack was estimated at 58 billion dollars and three months to clear the shipping backlog.[2] Much of the material that travels through U.S. ports does so quickly, is not inspected, and has an ambiguous chain of custody.

In light of the magnitude of this threat, President Bush issued National Security Presidential Directive-41/Homeland Security President Directive-13, "Maritime Security", directing several agencies to develop strategies, plans and programs to prevent and respond to threats from the maritime domain. Consequently, the Maritime Security Professionals Coordinating Committee (MSPCC) has developed the *National Strategy for Maritime Security* and several supporting plans including the interim *Maritime Operational Threat Response Plan*. These plans go a long way towards providing a better interagency coordination and cooperation framework to increase the security of the U.S. Maritime Domain.

Yet, despite all of the progress, the plans do not create or require an interagency Operation Center that is tasked with developing the U.S. Government response to a Maritime

---

[1] Department of Homeland Security, *Secure Seas Open Ports* (21 June 2005) <http://www.dhs.gov/ interweb/assetlibrary/DHSPortSecurityFactSheet-062104.pdf> [13 May 2006], 1.

[2] Mark Gerencser, Jim Weinberg, and Don Vincent, "Port Security War Game: Implications for the U.S. Supply Chains" (Booz, Allen, Hamilton, 2003), <http://www.boozallen.com/ media/file/128648.pdf> [15 May 2006], 1-2.

Domain threat. The United States needs such a center to effectively respond to and manage a Maritime Domain threat.

BACKGROUND

In the wake of the September 11, 2001 terrorist attacks, the formal requirements for Maritime Security have undergone much change. Recognizing the vulnerability the maritime domain presents to the United States, President Bush signed the "Maritime Security" *(NSPD-41)/(HSPD-13)* in December 2004.[3] NSPD-41/HSPD-13 "directs the coordination of United States Government maritime security programs and initiatives to achieve a cohesive national effort involving appropriate Federal, State, local, and private sector entities."[4] In light of the interagency complexity of the maritime security problem, NSPD-41/HSPD-13 also establishes the Maritime Security Policy Coordinating Committee (MSPCC), co-chaired by representatives from the National Security Council and the Homeland Security Council, to "coordinate interagency maritime security policy efforts."[5] Additionally, NSPD-41/HSPD-13 directs the Departments of Defense (DoD) and Homeland Security (DHS) to draft a National Maritime Security Strategy that "incorporate a global cross-discipline approach to the Maritime Domain centered on a layered, defense in depth framework that may be adjusted based on the threat level."[6] In response to this direction the MSPCC developed the *National Strategy for Maritime Security* along with its eight supporting plans including the *National Plan to Achieve Maritime Domain Awareness (MDA)* and the interim *Maritime Operational Threat Response Plan.*[7]

---

[3] President, Directive, "Maritime Security Policy," *National Security Presidential Directive NSPD-41/Homeland Security Presidential Directive HSPD-13* (Washington, D.C.: 21 December 2004), 1.
[4] Ibid., 1.
[5] Ibid., 1, 3.
[6] Ibid., 5.
[7] Department of Defense and Homeland Security, *National Strategy for Maritime Security* (Washington, D.C.: September 2005), ii.

Maritime Security involves a careful balancing act between defending the Maritime Domain against threats and allowing legitimate users to operate freely. The *National Strategy for Maritime Security* identifies that, "Nations have a common interest in achieving two complementary objectives: to facilitate the vibrant maritime commerce that underpins economic security, and to protect against ocean-related terrorist, hostile, criminal, and dangerous acts."[8] The dangers in the maritime domain might come from one of five types of threats: Nation-State Threats, Terrorist Threats, Transnational Criminal and Piracy Threats, Environmental Destruction and Illegal Seaborne Immigration.[9] The *National Strategy for Maritime Security* clearly identifies that the problem of maritime security is a vital national interest that is interagency and international in character. The NSMS has three broad principles: "preserve the freedom of the seas…facilitate and defend commerce…(and) facilitate the movement of desirable goods and people across our borders, while screening out dangerous people and material."[10] These principles are intended to guide the agencies as they work towards the following objectives of the *National Strategy for Maritime Security*:

- Prevent Terrorist Attacks and Criminal or Hostile Acts

- Protect Maritime-Related Population Centers and Critical Infrastructures

- Minimize Damage and Expedite Recovery

- Safeguard the Ocean and Its Resources[11]

Greater knowledge of the maritime domain is essential to provide Maritime Security. The *Plan to Achieve Maritime Domain Awareness* (MDA) is one of the seven supporting plans that is fundamental to establishing Maritime Security. The MDA plan is a roadmap

---

[8] Ibid., 2.
[9] Ibid., 3-6.
[10] Ibid., 7-8.
[11] Ibid., 8.

designed to develop "understanding of anything associated with the global Maritime Domain that could impact the security, safety, economy or environment of the United States."[12]

The *Maritime Operational Threat Response Plan* aims for "coordinated U.S. Government response to threats against the United States and its interests in the Maritime Domain" by establishing roles and responsibilities that enable the government to respond quickly and decisively.[13] To make this happen the *Maritime Operational Threat Response Plan* "directs the establishment of a network of integrated national-level maritime command centers, in order to achieve coordinated, unified, timely and effective U.S. Government Maritime Operational Threat Response (MOTR) planning and operational maritime command and control."[14] Yet, the plan stops short of establishing a unified maritime threat response center and directs that each agency's operations center establish communications links to the other MOTR agency's operations centers.[15] The MOTR plan designates the lead federal agency for various roles in maritime security. In this designation several areas of ambiguity remain. For instance, the Federal Bureau of Investigation (FBI) is designated the lead agency for "criminal investigation for all statutes within its jurisdiction arising from threats in the maritime domain and for all prosecutions arising from threats and/or acts in the maritime domain."[16] Yet the DHS is the lead agency for "criminal investigations for all statues within its jurisdiction arising from threats in the maritime domain."[17]

DoD doctrine is also not very clear as to which agency takes the lead for Maritime Security threats. *Joint Doctrine for Homeland Security* addresses the Maritime Security area

---

[12] President, 5.

[13] Department of Defense and Homeland Security, *National Strategy for Maritime Security: Maritime Operational Threat Response Plan* (Washington, D.C.: October 2005), 2.

[14] Ibid., 2.

[15] Ibid., 9.

[16] Ibid., 7.

[17] Ibid., 7.

under the missions of Homeland Security and Homeland Defense. DoD has the lead responsibility for a threat if that is determined to be a Homeland Defense mission. If the threat is a Homeland Security mission, DoD provides Civilian Support to the Lead Federal Agency (LFA). This construct holds for threats from the Maritime Domain as well as the air or land domains. When there is any confusion about whether a situation falls under the mission of Homeland Defense or Homeland Security, the President is the arbitrator who makes the decision.[18]

The guiding doctrine and requirements in the area of Maritime Security continues to develop. The *National Strategy for Maritime Security* directs the MSPCC to conduct a study with Departments of Justice, Homeland Security and Defense to determine the effectiveness of the network of interrelated operational command centers and develop "recommendations concerning the designation of an interagency planning and command and control entity to ensure unity of command for national execution of maritime security policy."[19] The current procedures for interagency coordination and decision-making do not include collocation of MOTR agency personnel at a single operations center.

DISCUSSION / ANALYSIS

Managing the Maritime Operational Threat

Determining the exact nature of a Maritime Operational Threat and the appropriate national response requires collaboration across multiple agencies and foreign governments, a consolidated intelligence picture, and a coordinated response to collect additional intelligence. Usually a terrorist attack from the Maritime Domain is considered the threat of

---

[18] Joint Chiefs of Staff, *Joint Doctrine for Homeland Security,* Joint Pub 3-26 (Washington, D.C.: 2 August 2005), 1-4.

[19] Department of Defense and Homeland Security, *National Strategy for Maritime Security: Maritime Operational Threat Response Plan,* 13.

most severe consequence. Terrorists have the capability and intent to use the Maritime

Domain in a number of ways. Terrorists may use the Maritime Domain to launch an attack

against the shipping infrastructure or the population centers located near these shipping

terminals. This type of attack may use conventional explosives or weapons of mass

destruction (WMD). In 2003, after noticing that it was zigzagging across the Mediterranean,

Greek authorities apprehended a ship that was loaded with 680 metric tons of ammonia

nitrate and 8000 detonators.[20] The Greek government had to have a mechanism to monitor

the ship and determine that its actions were suspicious and decide to board it. As Michael

Richardson explains, attacks of this nature will not only cause significant direct damage but

will also cause significant secondary effects including disruption of the global shipping

system that will cost billions of dollars to the global economy.[21] Terrorist may also use the

commercial shipping system to transport materials to construct weapons that could later be

used against the United States.

Determining the correct response to a maritime threat is challenging. The Maritime

Security agencies are assigned the objective to "detect, deter, interdict and defeat terrorist

attacks, criminal acts, or hostile acts in the maritime domain and prevent its unlawful

exploitation for those purposes.[22] At the same time the same agencies are to be guided by

the underlying principles of "facilitating and defending commerce…[and] facilitate the flow

of goods and resources across our borders."[23] Balancing the conflicting requirements to deter

and defend against threats from the Maritime Domain while maintaining the efficient flow of

goods and resources that is so critical to the world economy is challenging. It requires in-

---

[20] Michael Richardson, *A Time Bomb for Global Trade* (Singapore: Institute of Southeast Asian Studies, 2004), 45-46.

[21] Ibid., 66-71.

[22] Department of Defense and Homeland Security, *National Strategy for Maritime Security,* 8.

[23] Department of Defense and Homeland Security, *National Strategy for Maritime Security,* 7-8.

depth understanding of the traffic in the Maritime Domain and a carefully coordinated response to identify and direct the correct form of any interdiction and inspection actions.

To complicate matters further, most of the ships visiting U.S. ports are foreign flagged. Advanced inspection and interdiction of suspect vessels requires coordination with multiple agencies and foreign governments to determine which ships to intercept and the nature of the threat in each. The changing nature of the threat in the Maritime Domain also complicates the task of Maritime Security. The United States response to a threat from the maritime domain must cover the spectrum from diplomacy to law enforcement to military action. Initiatives such as the Department of State's Proliferation Security Initiative[24], Department of Homeland Security's Container Security Initiative[25] and Department of Energy's Megaport[26] program require voluntary cooperation of our international partners to collect information about cargo and vessels in the Maritime Domain. Coordinating the actions of distinct federal agencies across the spectrum of possible threats and responses is best done with a cross agency team working face-to-face in a real operational command center. Only with such a command center can the nation be assured that maritime threats will be met with the response that is best aligned with the interests of the nation and not one dominant agency.

Advantages of a Maritime Operational Threat Response Center

The United States requires a national operations center focused on Maritime Security threats across the spectrum, a Maritime Operational Threat Response Center (MOTRC).

---

[24] Department of State, "Proliferation Security Initiative: Statement of Interdiction Principles" Fact Sheet, 4 September 2003, <http://www.state.gov/t/isn/rls/fs/23764.htm> [13 May 2006].
[25] Department of Homeland Security, *Secure Seas Open Ports*, 5.
[26] Government Accountability Office, *Preventing Nuclear Smuggling: DOE Has Made Limited Progress in Installing Radiation Detection Equipment at Highest Priority Foreign Seaports*, GAO-05-375 (Washington, D.C.: March 2005).

MOTRC should be staffed with representatives from all relevant MOTR agencies. The operations center would have real time communications to all MOTR agencies national command centers and would develop the coordinated national policy and operational response to a maritime security threat. Advantages of a MOTRC include real time information sharing across agencies, situational awareness of maritime security information and a staff dedicated to analyze and characterize the nature of a threat, a single center dedicated to plan and develop procedures for responding to real-time maritime threats, the ability to develop policy and operational response to a threat in time to avoid the situation blooming into a crisis, and elimination of operational seams that might develop between agencies in the Maritime Domain.

Interaction in a face-to-face environment has distinct advantages that are conducive to effective management of the sort of issues that will arise while managing the MOTR. A report of research literature by Wainfan and Davis of the Rand research institute identified differences between groups that collaborate via video and audio conferencing and those that collaborate in a face-to-face setting. The study found that video and audio conferencing was more formal and better suited for groups that needed to make decisions based on well-established facts.[27] Face-to-face groups had higher levels of trust, greater participation and more cohesion with the groups.[28] The study also found that audio conferencing and video conferencing increased the formation of local coalitions that were biased against the groups at the other end of the line.[29] Additionally, the study concluded that the groups using audio

---

[27] Lynne Wainfan and Paul K. Davis, *Challenges in Virtual Collaboration* (Santa Monica: RAND, 2004), 19-23.
[28] Ibid., 19-23.
[29] Ibid., 33-34.

conference were less effective at tasks that required negotiation and cooperation.[30] These results indicate that an interagency group would be more capable of bridging the gap between agencies in a face-to-face setting while the members could maintain liaison with their parent agency via virtual communications methods. Finally, face-to-face interaction best fits a dynamic situation that will have high levels of uncertainty.

Knowledge is essential to managing the Maritime Security problem. Maritime Security professionals cannot defend against threats they do not know about. The *National Strategy for Maritime Security* defines Maritime Domain Awareness (MDA) as the "effective understanding of anything associated with the global maritime domain that could impact the security, safety, economy or environment of the United States."[31] MDA is an ambitious state of understanding that will require robust "collection, integration and dissemination of intelligence."[32] Although the plan to achieve MDA focuses on the technological systems that collect and present the Common Operating Picture, analysis of this data is required to generate knowledge and understanding. As the MDA system becomes more mature, information will be more readily available to Maritime Security professionals. Increased information availability will increase the need to coordinate the response to potential threats and follow up on leads. Security professionals know that intelligence must be processed by labor intensive investigation that requires significant manpower. The National Security Agency (NSA) and FBI ran into this phenomenon when they were sharing intelligence in the wake of the September 11th terrorist attacks. The NSA started sending the FBI suspected names, emails and phone numbers from the NSA electronic collection program. The FBI

---

[30] Ibid., 38.
[31] Department of Defense and Homeland Security, *National Strategy for Maritime Security: Plan to Achieve Maritime Domain Awareness,* 1.
[32] Ibid., 1.

became swamped with the additional workload required to follow up on each of these leads.[33] A more robust MDA system will produce information such as abnormal ship tracks and suspected inspection results that will require investigation. Although the MDA Plan anticipates that computer data analysis and integration algorithms will assist in processing the disparate data streams, operational decision makers will still be required to analyze the resulting data picture.[34] Coordinating the national government policy response to this information will require an interagency cooperation and collaboration. This type of work will be accomplished more efficiently in a real time collaboration center.

Truly transparent MDA is still many years in the future. A partial MDA picture will increase the need for information processing and follow-up at a command center like the MOTRC. The Department of Energy (DoE) Megaports program provides a relevant example. The DoE has been installing radiation detectors in foreign ports to monitor containers for shipments of undocumented radioactive material that may be used in a nuclear weapon. The program has become stalled because of host country resistance to accepting the devices. These countries are reluctant to accept an inspection regime that may slow down trade through their ports.[35] Additionally, incorrect operation of these devices or a lack of proper follow-up can result in a flurry of activity. Some ambiguous information was received from a recent installation of this detection equipment in Sri Lanka that had not been brought fully online. The resulting investigation identified as many as seventeen containers that may be carrying undocumented nuclear material on fourteen vessels.[36] The subsequent

---

[33] Lowell Bergman, Eric Lichtblau, Scott Shane and Don Van Natta Jr., "Spy Agency Data After Sept. 11 Led F.B.I. to Dead Ends," *New York Times*, 17 January 2006, sec 1A, 1.

[34] Department of Defense and Homeland Security, *National Strategy for Maritime Security: Plan to Achieve Maritime Domain Awareness*, 3.

[35] Government Accountability Office, 3-4.

[36] Interagency Team. "After Action Report on The Sri Lanka Neutron Alarm," unpublished report 24 January 2006, 1.

international response to track down and confirm the contents of each container highlights the need for a coordinated interagency and international response to the further investigation of intelligence tips in the Maritime Domain. An After Action Report produced by an interagency team, identified several lessons learned including establishing a "process for sharing Restricted Data with individuals with a need-to-know but without a DOE Q clearance"[37] and taking steps to "improve decision-making by developing case management tools that support interagency planning, communications, and improve situational awareness."[38] A consolidated MOTRC would allow simplified procedures for controlling access to sensitive information across agencies. Additionally, the MOTRC mission would be to improve decision making across the MOTR agencies with regard to the nuclear material threat as well as other dangerous materials. The MOTRC would allow sharing information without compromising information assurance or security requirements. In the Sri Lanka case, much of the information was shared over the Internet even though it was sensitive or classified.[39] The participants were forced to relax information security procedures to ensure relevant personnel had access to what they needed to know. The MOTRC could resolve these information access issues in advance and ensure that participants are brought into the loop at the appropriate time.

The Sri Lanka After Action Report also recommends "that agencies work to institutionalize interagency coordination and cooperation, with a view toward understanding organizational capabilities, authorities, and responsibilities to resolve alarms and to address

---

[37] Ibid., 7.
[38] Ibid., 7.
[39] Ibid., 11.

potential and real threats."[40] What better institution to promote interagency coordination and cooperation than the MOTRC?

The 9/11 Commission Report highlights the need to share intelligence information across agencies using a decentralized network model.[41] The 9/11 Commission refers to a model developed by the Markle Foundation to share information across a network of federal agencies, state and local government and the private sector.[42] Although, a virtual network may be required to expose all of the players to the MDA knowledge base, a full time staff that processes and categorizes information in an operations center will improve the effectiveness of such a network and ensure that appropriate processes for safeguarding information are implemented.

The MOTR plan "directs the establishment of a network of integrated national-level maritime command centers, in order to achieve coordinated, unified, timely and effective U.S. Government maritime operational threat response planning and operational maritime command and control."[43] The MOTR plan establishes procedures for interagency decision making between agency representatives that are not working in the same physical location. Establishing a MOTRC staffed by representatives from each of the MOTR agencies would accomplish the requirements of the national MOTR plan. The staff members would be the most effective structure to achieve coordinated, unified, timely and effective operational planning and operational maritime command and control in response to maritime operational threats.

---

[40] Ibid., 5.

[41] *The 9/11 Commission Report: Final Report of the National Commission on Terrorist Attacks Upon the United States* (New York, NY: Norton, 2004), 418.

[42] Zoe Baird and James Barksdale, *Creating a Trusted Information Network for Homeland Security* (Markle Foundation, December 2003), <http://www.markle.org/markle_programs/policy_for_a_networked_society/ national_security/projects/taskforce_national_security.php#report1> [9 May 2006], 2-3.

[43] Ibid., 2.

Appropriate MOTR planning requires operational practice and experimentation to develop robust procedures for responding to maritime operational threats. The Sri Lanka report recommends, "regular interagency exercises be conducted in order to improve and institutionalize interagency coordination and cooperation."[44] Additionally the MOTR Plan requires that DoD and DHS jointly lead MOTR exercises and make all efforts "to incorporate DOJ, DOS and foreign nation elements, in addition to other U.S. Government agencies, as required."[45] A MOTRC would provide the U.S. Government with the capability to develop and coordinate robust exercises with well-established measures of effectiveness to work out the procedures and protocols to respond to a Maritime Operational Threat. The MOTRC would be responsible for tracking corrective action identified from the exercises and real world events such as the Sri Lanka event and measuring progress towards improving the maritime threat response capability.

Once a potential maritime threat is identified, timely response is required to resolve the threat ambiguity and raise the level the threat or downgrade the threat as insignificant. Much of the response comes in the form of additional information gathering either from research or direct intelligence collection. Timely identification of intelligence requirements allows diplomatic channels to authorize collection of intelligence from suspect vessels without compromising any nation's sovereignty. The Sri Lanka event illustrates how delay in the initial response can raise the crisis level of a threat. With dedicated staffing effort in the MOTRC, requests for additional information can be made early to the appropriate collection activity and result in creation of a resolved Maritime Threat picture. Although a more robust MDA picture will help response personnel manage information about each maritime threat,

---

[44] Interagency Team, 8.

[45] Department of Defense and Homeland Security, *National Strategy for Maritime Security: Maritime Operational Threat Response Plan,* 13.

the MDA system will also highlight the unresolved maritime contacts that are potential threats. A MOTRC will be required to direct the collection of intelligence on these contacts or the response to the contacts as potential threats.

Integration of the domestic MOTR picture with the Combatant Commander's would also be a useful function of the MOTRC. In the Sri Lanka event, Central Command was not notified of several of the vessels of interest until they passed into European Command's Area of Responsibility (AOR). The Combatant Commander was denied the capability to craft an operational response to a potential maritime threat in his AOR. Although in this case the appropriate response would have been to maintain forces clear of the contacts while they transited the area, the Combatant Commander was not allowed the luxury of this limited response. The MOTR Plan requirement for a layered defense mandates that the Combatant Commander is a participant in the maritime security response.[46] The MOTRC can coordinate with the Combatant Commander Maritime Operation Center to allow the Combatant Commander to take the appropriate response that may include instituting appropriate force protection measures or contributing to the intelligence collection on the suspect vessel.

The Maritime Domain offers numerous seams between agencies and jurisdictions that complicate the U.S. Government response to a potential threat. As discussed above, the MOTR Plan tasks both the USCG and the FBI with law enforcement responsibilities in the Maritime Domain. There are numerous incidents where various national jurisdictions cross in the maritime domain as the location of the ship, flag country and the destination all give a country a claim to jurisdictional authority over the vessel. Finally, the USCG and the Navy have requirements to coordinate their response to maritime threats, particularly in the

---

[46] Ibid., 6.

approaches to the homeland. The MOTRC would provide a robust capability to resolve these seams and ensure that no terrorists are able to exploit them.

The decision about whether the response to a Maritime Threat is a Homeland Security or Homeland Defense mission is significant as it determines whether DoD is in the lead or not. Joint Doctrine determines that the President makes this decision if there is any confusion into which category a particular threat falls. The MOTRC would be the agency that consolidates the information on a maritime threat to give the President a unified picture to make this decision.

RECOMMENDATIONS

There are a number of issues that must be identified in organizing and aligning a MOTRC. Most interesting will be which agency operates the MOTRC, and whether it is aligned to a current operational command center. There is precedence for the design of the MOTC, an interagency operational center that processes information and takes operational command and control of the response to the threat. The MOTRC should be organized similar to the Joint Interagency Task Force-South (JIATF-South) attached to Southern Command that coordinates the efforts of federal, state and local law enforcement agencies such as the Drug Enforcement Agency and USCG to interdict drug trafficking.[47] Another example of an interagency team working with a Combatant Commander is Northern Command's Joint Task Force-6 that "supports counter-drug operations by federal, state and local law-enforcement agencies throughout the continental United States. It is being transformed into Joint Interagency Task Force North to engage all transnational threats-including terrorists-not just

---

[47] Congress, House, Committee on International Relations, Counternarcotics Strategies in Latin America: Hearing before the Subcommittee on Western Hemisphere, 109th Cong, 2nd sess., 30 March 2006, <http://www.dea.gov/pubs/cngrtest/ct033006.html> [9 May 2006].

drug smugglers."[48] The JIATF-South has proven that an interagency group can coordinate the complex response to a threat that crosses the realm of law enforcement and border security and has both a domestic and international flavor to it.[49]

Several other agencies outside of the DoD have command centers that could host the MOTRC. The DHS has recently stood up the Homeland Security Operations Center (HSOC). Its mission is to "integrate information sharing and domestic incident management."[50] Although a maritime section of the HSOC would be involved in a domestic response to maritime operational threat, it would most likely lack the international element to coordinate the defense in depth concept of the *National Strategy for Maritime Security*.

The Director of National Intelligence runs the National Counter Terrorism Center (NCTC). This center would be a significant player in the Maritime Operational Threat Response. The NCTC is serves as the intelligence integration and sharing point for counter terrorism and the strategic planning arm for the Global War on Terrorism. The NCTC is not tasked with integration with state and local agencies nor does it exercise operational command of forces.[51] Developing these capabilities would likely compromise the NCTC's ability to arbitrate the United State's intelligence analysis, sharing and collection priorities.

Regardless of which agency hosts the MOTRC, it will be critical that the center maintain the capability to operate without undue influence from the parent command. Organization under the Combatant Commander should not predicate a military response

---

[48] Harold Kennedy, "U.S. Northern Command Actively Enlisting Partners," *National Defense* 88, no. 607, (June 2004): 42, 44-45.

[49] Congress, House, Committee on International Relations.

[50] Department of Homeland Security, "Fact Sheet: Homeland Security Operations Center (HSOC)," <http://www.dhs.go/dhspublic/display?theme=43&content=3814&print =true4> [9 May 2006].

[51] Congress, House, Armed Services Committee, <u>Statement for the Record, The Honorable John Scott Redd, Director, National Counterterrorism Center</u>, 4 April 2006, <http://www.nctc.gov/press_room/speeches/20060404.html> [9 May 2006].

anymore than organization under the FBI should predicate strictly a law enforcement response to a maritime threat. The charter of the MOTRC must be clear in establishing its independence and operating character. The JIATF drug interdiction task force has been able to accomplish this and seems to be the best model.

CONCLUSION

Without an operational command center dedicated to MOTR the nation will trust the response to a threat in the maritime domain to the virtual collaboration between maritime security professionals of different agencies. Although technology will continue to provide tools to enhance the ability to conduct virtual collaboration the response will be degraded both in quality and timeliness. Without a dedicated team of professionals that can analyze potential Maritime Operational threats presented on the Common Operating Picture, true understanding described in the Plan for Maritime Domain Awareness will remain elusive.

Bibliography

Baird, Zoe and James Barksdale. *Creating a Trusted Information Network for Homeland Security.* Markle Foundation, December 2003. <http://www.markle.org/ markle_programs/policy_for_a_networked_society/national_security/projects/taskfor ce_national_security.php#report1> [9 May 2006].

Gerencser, Mark, Jim Weinberg, and Don Vincent. "Port Security War Game: Implications for the U.S. Supply Chains." Booz, Allen, Hamilton, 2003. <http://www.boozallen. com/media/file/128648.pdf> [15 May 2006].

Kennedy, Harold. "U.S. Northern Command Actively Enlisting Partners." *National Defense* 88, no. 607, (June 2004): 42,44-45.

The 9/11 Commission Report: Final Report of the National Commission on Terrorist Attacks Upon the United States. New York: Norton, 2004.

Richardson, Michael. *A Time Bomb for Global Trade.* Singapore: Institute of Southeast Asian Studies, 2004.

U.S. Congress. House. Armed Services Committee. Statement for the Record, The Honorable John Scott Redd, Director, National Counterterrorism Center. 4 April 2006. <http://www.nctc.gov/press_room/speeches/ 20060404.html> [9 May 2006].

U.S. Congress. House. Committee on International Relations. Counternarcotics Strategies in Latin America: Hearing before the Subcommittee on Western Hemisphere. 109th Cong, 2nd sess., 30 March 2006, <http://www.dea.gov/pubs/cngrtest/ct033006.html> [9 May 2006].

U.S. Department of Defense and Department of Homeland Security. *National Strategy for Maritime Security.* Washington, D.C.: September 2005.

U.S. Department of Defense and Homeland Security. *National Strategy for Maritime Security: Maritime Operational Threat Response Plan.* Washington, D.C.: October 2005.

U.S. Department of Homeland Security. "Fact Sheet: Homeland Security Operations Center (HSOC)." <http://www.dhs.go/dhspublic/display?theme=43&content=3814&print =true4> [9 May 2006].

U.S. Department of Homeland Security. *Secure Seas Open Ports.* 21 June 2005. <http://www.dhs.gov/ interweb/assetlibrary/DHSPortSecurityFactSheet-062104.pdf> [13 May 2006].

U.S. Department of State. "Proliferation Security Initiative: Statement of Interdiction Principles" Fact Sheet. 4 September 2003. <http://www.state.gov/t/isn/rls/fs/ 23764.htm> [13 May 2006].

U. S. Government Accountability Office. *Preventing Nuclear Smuggling: DOE Has Made Limited Progress in Installing Radiation Detection Equipment at Highest Priority Foreign Seaports.* Washington, D.C.: March 2005.

U.S. Interagency Team. "After Action Report on The Sri Lanka Neutron Alarm," unpublished report 24 January 2006.

U.S. Joint Chiefs of Staff. *Joint Doctrine for Homeland Security.* Joint Pub 3-26. Washington, D.C.: 2 August 2005.

U.S. President. Directive. "Maritime Security Policy." *National Security Presidential Directive NSPD-41/Homeland Security Presidential Directive HSPD-13.* Washington, D.C.: 21 December 2004.

Wainfan, Lynne and Paul K. Davis. *Challenges in Virtual Collaboration.* Santa Monica: RAND, 2004.